A Treatise on Grace and Free Will

A Treatise on Grace and Free Will

St. Augustine

A Treatise on Grace and Free Will

© Lighthouse Publishing 2018

Written by: St. Augustine (Nov.13 354 – Aug.28 430)
Translated by Peter Holmes and Robert Ernest Wallis
Revised by: Professor Benjamin B. Warfield, D.D
Updated into Modern U.S English by A.M. Overett (b. 1960)

All rights reserved. Without limiting the rights under copyright reserved above, no part of this publication may be reproduced, stored in a retrieval system, or transmitted, in any form or by any means (electronic, mechanical, photocopying, recording or otherwise), without the prior written permission of the copyright owner of this book.

Published by
Lighthouse Christian Publishing
SAN 257-4330
5531 Dufferin Drive
Savage, Minnesota, 55378
United States of America

www.lighthousechristianpublishing.com

EXTRACT FROM AUGUSTIN'S "RETRACTATIONS,"

Book II. Chap. 66,

ON THE FOLLOWING TREATISE, "DE GRATIA ET LIBERO ARBITRIO."

There are some persons who suppose that the freedom of the will is denied whenever God's grace is maintained, and who on their side defend their liberty of will so peremptorily as to deny the grace of God. This grace, as they assert, is bestowed according to our own merits. It is in consequence of their opinions that I wrote the book entitled On Grace and Free Will. This work I addressed to the monks of Adrumetum, in whose monastery first arose the controversy on that subject, and that in such a manner that some of them were obliged to consult me thereon. The work begins with these words: "With reference to those persons who so preach the liberty of the human will."

TWO LETTERS WRITTEN BY AUGUSTIN TO
VALENTINUS AND THE MONKS OF ADRUMETUM,
AND FORWARDED WITH THE FOLLOWING
TREATISE.

Letter I.

[The 214th of Augustin's Epistles.]

To my very dear lord and most honored brother among the members of Christ, Valentinus, and to the brethren that are with you, Augustin sends greeting in the Lord.

1. Two young men, Cresconius and Felix, have found their way to us, and, introducing themselves as belonging to your brotherhood, have told us that your monastery was disturbed with no small commotion, because certain amongst you preach grace in such a manner as to deny that the will of man is free; and maintain—a more serious matter—that in the day of judgment God will not render to every man according to his works. At the same time, they have pointed out to us, that many of you do not entertain this opinion, but allow that free will is assisted by the grace of God, so as that we may think and do aright; so that, when the Lord shall come to render unto every man according to his works, He shall find those works of ours good which God has prepared in order that we may walk in them. They who think this think rightly.

2. "I beseech you therefore, brethren," even as the apostle besought the Corinthians, "by the name of our Lord Jesus Christ, that ye all speak the same thing, and that there be no divisions among you." For, in the first place, the Lord Jesus, as it is written in the Gospel of the Apostle John, "came not to condemn the world, but that the world by Himself might be saved." Then, afterwards, as the Apostle Paul writes, "God shall judge the world when He shall come," as the whole Church confesses in

the Creed, "to judge the quick and the dead." Now, I would ask, if there is no grace of God, how does He save the world? and if there is no free will, how does He judge the world? That book of mine, therefore, or epistle, which the above-mentioned brethren have brought with them to you, I wish you to understand in accordance with this faith, so that you may neither deny God's grace, nor uphold free will in such wise as to separate the latter from the grace of God, as if without this we could by any means either think or do anything according to God,— which is quite beyond our power. On this account, indeed, it is, that the Lord when speaking of the fruits of righteousness said, "Without me ye can do nothing."

3. From this you may understand why I wrote the letter which has been referred to, to Sixtus, presbyter of the Church at Rome, against the new Pelagian heretics, who say that the grace of God is bestowed according to our own merits, so that he who glories has to glory not in the Lord, but in himself,—that is to say, in man, not in the Lord. This, however, the apostle forbids in these words: "Let no man glory in man;" while in another passage he says, "He that glories let him glory in the Lord." But these heretics, under the idea that they are justified by their own selves, just as if God did not bestow on them this gift, but they themselves obtained it by themselves, glory of course in themselves, and not in the Lord. Now, the apostle says to such, "Who makes thee to differ from another?" and this he does claiming out of the mass of perdition which arose from Adam, none but God distinguishes a man to make him a vessel to honors, and not to dishonor. Lest, however, the carnal man in his foolish pride should, on hearing the question, "Who makes thee to differ from another?" either in thought or in

word answer and say: My faith, or my prayer, or my righteousness makes me to differ from other men, the apostle at once adds these words to the question, and so meets all such notions, saying, "What hast thou that thou didst not receive? now, if thou didst receive it, why dost thou glory, as if thou didst not receive it?" Now, they boast as if they did not receive their gifts by grace, who think that they are justified of their own selves, and who, on this account, glory in themselves, and not in the Lord.

4. Therefore I have in this letter, which has reached you, shown by passages of Holy Scripture, which you can examine for yourselves, that our good works and pious prayers and right faith could not possibly have been in us unless we had received them all from Him, concerning whom the Apostle James says, "Every good gift and every perfect gift is from above, and cometh down from the Father of lights." And so no man can say that it is by the merit of his own works, or by the merit of his own prayers, or by the merit of his own faith, that God's grace has been conferred upon him; nor suppose that the doctrine is true which those heretics hold, that the grace of God is given us in proportion to our own merit. This is altogether a most erroneous opinion; not, indeed, because there is no desert, good in pious persons, or evil in impious ones (for how else shall God judge the world?), but because a man is converted by that mercy and grace of God, of which the Psalmist says, "As for my God, His mercy shall prevent me;" so that the unrighteous man is justified, that is, becomes just instead of impious, and begins to possess that good desert which God will crown when the world shall be judged.

5. There were many things which I wanted to send you, by the perusal whereof you would have been able to

gain a more exact and full knowledge of all that has been done by the bishops in their councils against these Pelagian heretics. But the brethren were in haste who came to us from your company. By them we have sent you this letter; which is, however, not an answer to any communication, because, in truth, they brought us no epistle from your beloved selves. Yet we had no hesitation in receiving them; for their simple manners proved to us clearly enough that there could have been nothing unreal or deceptive in their visit to us. They were, however, in much haste, as wishing to spend Easter at home with you; and my earnest prayer is, that so sacred a day may, by the Lord's help, bring peace to you, and not dissension.

6. You will, indeed, take the better course (as I earnestly request you), if you will not refuse to send to me the very person by whom they say they have been disturbed. For either he does not understand my book, or else, perhaps, he is himself misunderstood, when he endeavors to solve and explain a question which is a very difficult one, and intelligible to few. For it is none other than the question of God's grace which has caused persons of no understanding to think that the Apostle Paul prescribes it to us as a rule, "Let us do evil that good may come." It is in reference to these that the Apostle Peter writes in his second Epistle; "Wherefore, beloved, seeing that ye look for such things, be diligent, that ye may be found of Him in peace, without spot and blameless and account that the long-suffering of our Lord is salvation; even as our beloved brother Paul also, according to the wisdom given unto him, hath written unto you; as also in all his epistles, speaking in them of these things: in which are some things hard to be understood, which they that are

unlearned and unstable wrest, as they do also the other Scriptures, unto their own destruction."

7. Take good heed, then, to these fearful words of the great apostle; and when you feel that you do not understand, put your faith in the meanwhile in the inspired word of God, and believe both that man's will is free, and that there is also God's grace, without whose help man's free will can neither be turned towards God, nor make any progress in God. And what you piously believe, that pray that you may have a wise understanding of. And, indeed, it is for this very purpose, —that is, that we may have a wise understanding, that there is a free will. For unless we understood and were wise with a free will, it would not be enjoined to us in the words of Scripture, "Understand now, ye simple among the people; and ye fools, at length be wise." The very precept and injunction which calls on us to be intelligent and wise, requires also our obedience; and we could exercise no obedience without free will. But if it were in our power to obey this precept to be understanding and wise by free will, without the help of God's grace, it would be unnecessary to say to God, "Give me understanding, that I may learn Thy commandments;" nor would it have been written in the gospel, "Then opened He their understanding, that they might understand the Scriptures;" nor should the Apostle James address us in such words as, "If any of you lack wisdom, let him ask of God, who giveth to all men liberally, and upbraided not; and it shall be given him." But the Lord can grant, both to you and to us, that we may rejoice over very speedy tidings of your peace and pious unanimity. I send you greeting, not in my own name only, but of the brethren also who are with me;

and I ask you to pray for us with one accord and with all earnestness. The Lord be with you.

Letter II.

[The 215th of Augustin's Epistles.]

To my very dear lord and most honored brother among the members of Christ, Valentinus, and to the brethren that are with you, Augustin sends greeting in the Lord.

1. That Cresconius and Felix, and another Felix, the servants of God, who came to us from your brotherhood, have spent Easter with us is known to your Love. We have detained them some while longer in order that they might return to you better instructed against the new Pelagian heretics, into whose error everyone falls who supposes that it is according to any human merits that the grace of God is given to us, which alone delivers a man through Jesus Christ our Lord. But he, too, is no less in error who thinks that, when the Lord shall come to judgment, a man is not judged according to his works who has been able to use throughout his life free choice of will. For only infants, who have not yet done any works of their own, either good or bad, will be condemned because of original sin alone, when they have not been delivered by the Savior's grace in the laver of regeneration. As for all others who, in the use of their free will, have added to original sin, sins of their own commission, but who have not been delivered by God's grace from the power of darkness and removed into the kingdom of Christ, they will receive judgment according

to the deserts not of their original sin only, but also of the acts of their own will. The good, indeed, shall receive their reward according to the merits of their own good-will, but then they received this very good-will through the grace of God; and thus is accomplished that sentence of Scripture, "Indignation and wrath, tribulation and anguish, upon every soul of man that doeth evil, of the Jew first, and also of the Gentile: but glory, honors, and peace to every man that worketh good; to the Jew first, and also to the Gentile."

2. Touching the very difficult question of will and grace, I have felt no need of treating it further in this letter, having given them another letter also when they were about to return in greater haste. I have written a book likewise for you, and if you, by the Lord's help, read it, and have a lively understanding of it, I think that no further dissension on this subject will arise among you. They take with them other documents besides, which, as we supposed, ought to be sent to you, in order that from these you may ascertain what means the catholic Church has adopted for repelling, in God's mercy, the poison of the Pelagian heresy. For the letters to Pope Innocent, Bishop of Rome, from the Council of the province of Carthage, and from the Council of Numidia, and one written with exceeding care by five bishops, and what he wrote back to these three; our letter also to Pope Zosimus about the African Council, and his answer addressed to all bishops throughout the world; and a brief constitution, which we drew up against the error itself at a later plenary Council of all Africa; and the above-mentioned book of mine, which I have just written for you,—all these we have both read over with them, while they were with us, and have now dispatched by their hands to you.

3. Furthermore, we have read to them the work of the most blessed martyr Cyprian on the Lord's Prayer, and have pointed out to them how He taught that all things pertaining to our morals, which constitute right living, must be sought from our Father which is in heaven, lest, by presuming on free will, we fall from divine grace. From the same treatise we have also shown them how the same glorious martyr has taught us that it behooves us to pray even for our enemies who have not yet believed in Christ, that they may believe; which would of course be all in vain unless the Church believed that even the evil and unbelieving wills of men might, by the grace of God, be converted to good. This book of St. Cyprian, however, we have not sent you, because they told us that you possessed it among yourselves already. My letter, also, which had been sent to Sixtus, presbyter of the Church at Rome and which they brought with them to us, we read over with them, and pointed out how that it had been written in opposition to those who say that God's grace is bestowed according to our merits,—that is to say, in opposition to the same Pelagians.

4. As far, then, as lay in our power, we have used our influence with them, as both your brethren and our own, with a view to their persevering in the soundness of the catholic faith, which neither denies free will whether for an evil or a good life, nor attributes to it so much power that it can avail anything without God's grace, whether that it may be changed from evil to good, or that it may persevere in the pursuit of good, or that it may attain to eternal good when there is no further fear of failure. To yourselves, too, my most dearly beloved, I also, in this letter, give the same exhortation which the apostle addresses to us all, "not to think of yourselves

more highly than you ought to think; but to think soberly, according as God hath dealt to every man the measure of faith."

5. Mark well the counsel which the Holy Ghost gives us by Solomon: "Make straight paths for thy feet and order thy ways aright. Turn not aside to the right hand nor to the left, but turn away thy foot from the evil way; for the Lord knows the ways on the right hand, but those on the left are perverse. He will make thy ways straight and will direct thy steps in peace." Now consider, my brethren, that in these words of Holy Scripture, if there were no free will, it would not be said, "Make straight paths for thy feet, and order thy ways; turn not aside to the right hand, nor to the left." Nor yet, were this possible for us to achieve without the grace of God, would it be afterwards added, "He will make thy ways straight, and will direct thy steps in peace."

6. Decline, therefore, neither to the right hand nor to the left, although the paths on the right hand are praised, and those on the left hand are blamed. Therefore he added, "Turn away thy foot from the evil way,"—that is, from the left-hand path. This he makes manifest in the following words, saying, "For the Lord knows the ways on the right hand; but those on the left are perverse." In those ways we ought surely to walk which the Lord knows; and it is of these that we read in the Psalm, "The Lord knows the way of the righteous, but the way of the ungodly shall perish;" for this way, which is on the left hand, the Lord does not know. As He will also say at last to such as are placed on His left hand at the day of judgment: "I know you not." Now what is that which He knows not, who knows all things, both good and evil, in man? But what is the meaning of the words, "I know you

not," unless it be that you are now such as I never made you? Precisely as that passage runs, which is spoken of the Lord Jesus Christ, that "He knew no sin." How knew it not, except that He had never made it? And, therefore, how is to be understood the passage, "The ways which are on the right hand the Lord knows," except in the sense that He made those ways Himself,—even "the paths of the righteous," which no doubt are "those good works that God," as the apostle tells us, "hath before ordained that we should walk in them"? Whereas the left-hand ways—those perverse paths of the unrighteous—He truly knows nothing of, because He never made them for man, but man made them for himself. Wherefore He says, "The perverse ways of the wicked I utterly abhor; they are on the left hand."

7. But the reply is made: Why did He say, "Turn not aside to the right hand, nor to the left," when he clearly ought rather to have said, Keep to the right hand, and turn not off to the left, if the right-hand paths are good? Why, do we think, except this, that the paths on the right hand are so good that it is not good to turn off from them, even to the right? For that man, indeed, is to be understood as declining to the right who chooses to attribute to himself, and not to God, even those good works which appertain to right-hand ways. Hence it was that after saying, "For the Lord knows the ways on the right hand, but those on the left hand are perverse," as if the objection were raised to Him, Wherefore, then, do you not wish us to turn aside to the right? He immediately added as follows: "He will Himself make thy paths straight, and will direct thy ways in peace." Understand, therefore, the precept, "Make straight paths for thy feet, and order thy ways aright," in such a sense as to know

that whenever you do all this, it is the Lord God who enables you to do it. Then you will not turn off to the right, although you are walking in right-hand paths, not trusting in your own strength; and He will Himself be your strength, who will make straight paths for your feet, and will direct your ways in peace.

8. Wherefore, most dearly beloved, whosoever says, My will suffices for me to perform good works, declines to the right. But, on the other hand, they who think that a good way of life should be forsaken, when they hear God's grace so preached as to lead to the supposition and belief that it of itself makes men's wills from evil to good, and it even of itself keeps them what it has made them; and who, as the result of this opinion, go on to say, "Let us do evil that good may come,"—these persons decline to the left. This is the reason why he said to you, "Turn not aside to the right hand, nor to the left;" in other words, do not uphold free will in such wise as to attribute good works to it without the grace of God, nor so defend and maintain grace as if, by reason of it, you may love evil works in security and safety,—which may God's grace itself avert from you! Now it was the words of such as these which the apostle had in view when he said, "What shall we say, then? Shall we continue in sin that grace may abound?" And to this cavil of erring men, who know nothing about the grace of God, he returned such an answer as he ought in these words: "God forbid. How shall we, that are dead to sin, live any longer therein?" Nothing could have been said more succinctly, and yet to the point. For what more useful gift does the grace of God confer upon us, in this present evil world, than our dying unto sin? Hence he shows himself ungrateful to grace itself who chooses to live in sin by reason of that whereby

we die unto sin. May God, however, who is rich in mercy, grant you both to think soundly and wisely, and to continue perseveringly and progressively to the end in every good determination and purpose. For yourselves, for us, for all who love you, and for those who hate you, pray that this gift may be attained, —pray earnestly and vigilantly in brotherly peace. Live unto God. If I deserve any favor at your hands, let brother Florus come to me.

St. Augustine

A TREATISE ON GRACE AND FREE WILL, BY AURELIUS AUGUSTIN, BISHOP OF HIPPO; addressed to Valentinus and the monks of Adrumetum, and completed in one book. written in a.d. 426 or a.d. 427

In this treatise Augustin teaches us to beware of maintaining grace by denying free will, or free will by denying grace; for that it is evident from the testimony of Scripture that there is in man a free choice of will; and there are also in the same Scriptures inspired proofs given of that very grace of God without which we can do nothing good. Afterwards, in opposition to the Pelagians, he proves that grace is not bestowed according to our merits. He explains how eternal life, which is rendered to good works, is really of grace. He then goes on to show that the grace which is given to us through our Lord Jesus Christ is neither the knowledge of the law, nor nature, nor simply remission of sins; but that it is grace that makes us fulfil the law, and causes nature to be liberated from the dominion of sin. He demolishes that vain subterfuge of the Pelagians, to the effect that "grace, although it is not bestowed according to the merits of good works, is yet given according to the merits of the antecedent good-will of the man who believes and prays." He incidentally touches the question, why God commands what He means Himself to give, and whether He imposes on us any commands which we are unable to perform. He clearly shows that the love which is indispensable for fulfilling the commandments is only within us from God Himself. He points out that God works in men's hearts to incline their wills whithersoever He wills, either to good works according to His mercy, or to evil ones in return for their deserving; His judgment, indeed, being sometimes manifest, sometimes hidden, but always righteous. Lastly, he teaches us that a clear example of the gratuitousness of grace, not given in return for our deserts, is supplied to us in the case of those infants which are saved, while others perish though their case is identical with that of the rest.

Chapter 1 [I.]—The Occasion and Argument of This Work.

With reference to those persons who so preach and defend man's free will, as boldly to deny, and endeavor to do away with, the grace of God which calls us to Him, and delivers us from our evil deserts, and by which we obtain the good deserts which lead to everlasting life: we have already said a good deal in discussion, and committed it to writing, so far as the Lord has vouchsafed to enable us. But since there are some persons who so defend God's grace as to deny man's free will, or who suppose that free will is denied when grace is defended, I have determined to write somewhat on this point to your Love, my brother Valentinus, and the rest of you, who are serving God together under the impulse of a mutual love. For it has been told me concerning you, brethren, by some members of your brotherhood who have visited us, and are the bearers of this communication of ours to you, that there are dissensions among you on this subject. This, then, being the case, dearly beloved, that you be not disturbed by the obscurity of this question, I counsel you first to thank God for such things as you understand; but as for all which is beyond the reach of your mind, pray for understanding from the Lord, observing, at the same time peace and love among yourselves; and until He Himself lead you to perceive what at present is beyond your comprehension, walk firmly on the ground of which you are sure. This is the advice of the Apostle Paul, who, after saying that he was not yet perfect, a little later adds, "Let us, therefore, as many as are perfect, be thus minded,"— meaning perfect to a certain extent, but not having attained to a perfection sufficient for us; and then immediately adds, "And if, in anything, ye be otherwise minded, God shall reveal even this unto you. Nevertheless, whereunto we have already attained, let us walk by the same rule." For by walking in what we have attained, we shall be able to advance to what we have not yet attained, —God revealing it to us if in anything we are otherwise minded, —provided we do not give up what He has already revealed.

Chapter 2 [II.]—He Proves the Existence of Free Will in Man from the Precepts Addressed to Him by God.

Now He has revealed to us, through His Holy Scriptures, that there is in a man a free choice of will. But how He has revealed this I do not recount in human language, but in divine. There is, to begin with, the fact that God's precepts themselves would be of no use to a man unless he had free choice of will, so that by performing them he might obtain the promised rewards. For they are given that no one might be able to plead the excuse of ignorance, as the Lord says concerning the Jews in the gospel: "If I had not come and spoken unto them, they would not have sin; but now they have no excuse for their sin." Of what sin does He speak but of that great one which He foreknew, while speaking thus, that they would make their own—that is, the death they were going to inflict upon Him? For they did not have "no sin" before Christ came to them in the flesh. The apostle also says: "The wrath of God is revealed from heaven against all ungodliness and unrighteousness of men who hold back the truth in unrighteousness; because that which may be known of God is manifest in them; for God hath showed it unto them. For the invisible things of Him are from the creation of the world clearly seen—being understood by the things that are made—even His eternal power and Godhead, so that they are inexcusable." In what sense does he pronounce them to be "inexcusable," except with reference to such excuse as human pride is apt to allege in such words as, "If I had only known, I would have done it; did I not fail to do it because I was ignorant of it?" or, "I would do it if I knew how; but I do not know, therefore I do not do it"? All such excuse is removed from them when the precept is given them, or the knowledge is made manifest to them how to avoid sin.

Chapter 3. —Sinners are Convicted When Attempting to Excuse Themselves by Blaming God, Because They Have Free Will.

There are, however, persons who attempt to find excuse for themselves even from God. The Apostle James says to such: "Let no man say when he is tempted, I am tempted of God; for God cannot be tempted with evil, neither tempted He any man. But every man is tempted when he is drawn away of his own lust and enticed. Then, when lust hath conceived, it brings forth sin: and sin, when it is finished, brings forth death." Solomon, too, in his book of Proverbs, has this answer for such as wish to find an excuse for themselves from God Himself: "The folly of a man spoils his ways; but he blames God in his heart." And in the book of Ecclesiasticus we read: "Say not thou, It is through the Lord that I fell away; for thou ought not to do the things that He hated: nor do thou say, He hath caused me to err; for He hath no need of the sinful man. The Lord hated all abomination, and they that fear God love it not. He Himself made man from the beginning and left him in the hand of His counsel. If thou be willing, thou shalt keep His commandments, and perform true fidelity. He hath set fire and water before thee: stretch forth thine hand unto whether thou wilt. Before man is life and death, and whichsoever pleased him shall be given to him." Observe how very plainly is set before our view the free choice of the human will.

Chapter 4. —The Divine Commands Which are Most Suited to the Will Itself Illustrate Its Freedom.

What is the import of the fact that in so many passages God requires all His commandments to be kept and fulfilled? How does He make this requisition, if there is no free will? What means "the happy man," of whom the Psalmist says that "his will has been the law of the Lord"? Does he not clearly enough show that a man by his own will takes his stand in the law of God? Then again, there are so many commandments which in some way are expressly adapted to the human will; for instance, there is, "Be not overcome of evil," and others of similar import, such as, "Be not like a horse or a mule, which have no understanding;" and, "Reject not the counsels of thy mother;" and, "Be not wise in thine own conceit;" and, "Despise not the chastening of the Lord;" and,

"Forget not my law;" and, "Forbear not to do good to the poor;" and, "Devise not evil against thy friend;" and, "Give no heed to a worthless woman;" and, "He is not inclined to understand how to do good;" and, "They refused to attend to my counsel;" with numberless other passages of the inspired Scriptures of the Old Testament. And what do they all show us but the free choice of the human will? So, again, in the evangelical and apostolic books of the New Testament what other lesson is taught us? As when it is said, "Lay not up for yourselves treasures upon earth;" and, "Fear not them which kill the body;" and, "If any man will come after me, let him deny himself;" and again, "Peace on earth to men of good will." So also that the Apostle Paul says: "Let him do what he wills; he sinned not if he marry. Nevertheless, he that stands steadfast in his heart, having no necessity, but hath power over his own will, and hath so decreed in his heart that he will keep his virgin, doeth well." And so again, "If I do this willingly, I have a reward;" while in another passage he says, "Be ye sober and righteous, and sin not;" and again, "As ye have a readiness to will, so also let there be a prompt performance;" then he remarks to Timothy about the younger widows, "When they have begun to wax wanton against Christ, they choose to marry." So in another passage, "All that will to live godly in Christ Jesus shall suffer persecution;" while to Timothy himself he says, "Neglect not the gift that is in thee." Then to Philemon he addresses this explanation: "That thy benefit should not be as it were of necessity, but of thine own will." Servants also he advises to obey their masters "with a good will." In strict accordance with this, James says: "Do not err, my beloved brethren . . . and have not the faith of our Lord Jesus Christ with respect to persons;"

and, "Do not speak evil one of another." So also John in his Epistle writes, "Do not love the world," and other things of the same import. Now wherever it is said, "Do not do this," and "Do not do that," and wherever there is any requirement in the divine admonitions for the work of the will to do anything, or to refrain from doing anything, there is at once a sufficient proof of free will. No man, therefore, when he sins, can in his heart blame God for it, but every man must impute the fault to himself. Nor does it detract at all from a man's own will when he performs any act in accordance with God. Indeed, a work is then to be pronounced a good one when a person does it willingly; then, too, may the reward of a good work be hoped for from Him concerning whom it is written, "He shall reward every man according to his works."

Chapter 5. —He Shows that Ignorance Affords No Such Excuse as Shall Free the Offender from Punishment; But that to Sin with Knowledge is a Graver Thing Than to Sin in Ignorance.

The excuse such as men are in the habit of alleging from ignorance is taken away from those persons who know God's commandments. But neither will those be without punishment who know not the law of God. "For as many as have sinned without law shall also perish without law; and as many as have sinned in the law shall be judged by the law." Now the apostle does not appear to me to have said this as if he meant that they would have to suffer something worse who in their sins are ignorant of the law than they who know it. [III.] It is seemingly worse, no doubt, "to perish" than "to be judged;" but inasmuch as he was speaking of the Gentiles and of the

Jews when he used these words, because the former were without the law, but the latter had received the law, who can venture to say that the Jews who sin in the law will not perish, since they refused to believe in Christ, when it was of them that the apostle said, "They shall be judged by the law"? For without faith in Christ no man can be delivered; and therefore, they will be so judged that they perish. If, indeed, the condition of those who are ignorant of the law of God is worse than the condition of those who know it, how can that be true which the Lord says in the gospel: "The servant who knows not his lord's will, and commits things worthy of stripes, shall be beaten with few stripes; whereas the servant who knows his lord's will, and commits things worthy of stripes, shall be beaten with many stripes"? Observe how clearly He here shows that it is a graver matter for a man to sin with knowledge than in ignorance. And yet we must not on this account betake ourselves for refuge to the shades of ignorance, with the view of finding our excuse therein. It is one thing to be ignorant, and another thing to be unwilling to know. For the will is at fault in the case of the man of whom it is said, "He is not inclined to understand, so as to do good." But even the ignorance, which is not theirs who refuse to know, but theirs who are, as it were, simply ignorant, does not so far excuse any one as to exempt him from the punishment of eternal fire, though his failure to believe has been the result of his not having at all heard what he should believe; but probably only so far as to mitigate his punishment. For it was not said without reason: "Pour out Thy wrath upon the heathen that have not known Thee;" nor again according to what the apostle says: "When He shall come from heaven in a flame of fire to take vengeance on them that know not God." But yet in order that we may have that knowledge that will prevent our saying, each one of us, "I did not know," "I did not hear," "I did not understand;" the human will is summoned, in such words as these: "Wish not to be as the horse or as the mule, which have no understanding;" although it may show itself even worse, of which it is written, "A stubborn servant will not be reproved by words; for even if he understand, yet he will not obey." But when a man says, "I cannot do what I am commanded, because I am mastered by my concupiscence," he has no longer any excuse to plead from ignorance, nor reason to blame God in his heart, but he recognizes and laments his own evil in himself; and still to such an one the apostle says: "Be not overcome by evil, but overcome evil with good;" and of course the very fact that the injunction, "Consent not to be overcome," is addressed to him, undoubtedly summons the determination of his will. For to consent and to refuse are functions proper to will.

Chapter 6 [IV.]—God's Grace to Be Maintained Against the Pelagians; The Pelagian Heresy Not an Old One.

It is, however, to be feared lest all these and similar testimonies of Holy Scripture (and undoubtedly there are a great many of them), in the maintenance of free will, be understood in such a way as to leave no room for God's assistance and grace in leading a godly life and a good conversation, to which the eternal reward is due; and lest poor wretched man, when he leads a good life and performs good works (or rather thinks that he leads a good life and performs good works), should dare to glory in himself and not in the Lord, and to put his hope of righteous living in himself alone; so as to be followed by the prophet Jeremiah's malediction when he says, "Cursed is the man who has hope in man, and makes strong the flesh of his arm, and whose heart departed from the Lord." Understand, my brethren, I pray you, this passage of the prophet. Because the prophet did not say, "Cursed is the man who has hope in his own self," it might seem to some that the passage, "Cursed is the man who has hope in man," was spoken to prevent man having hope in any other man but himself. In order, therefore, to show that his admonition to man was not to have hope in himself, after saying, "Cursed is the man who has hope in man," he immediately added, "And makes strong the flesh of his arm." He used the word "arm" to designate power in operation. By the term "flesh," however, must be understood human frailty. And therefore he makes strong the flesh of his arm who supposes that a power which is frail and weak (that is, human) is sufficient for him to perform good works, and therefore puts not his hope in God for help. This is the reason why he subjoined the further clause, "And whose heart departed from the Lord." Of this character is the Pelagian heresy, which is not an ancient one, but has only lately come into existence. Against this system of error there was first a good deal of discussion; then, as the ultimate resource, it was referred to sundry episcopal councils, the proceedings of which, not, indeed, in every instance, but in some, I have dispatched to you for your perusal. In order, then, to our performance of good works, let us not have hope in man, making strong the flesh of our arm; nor let our heart ever depart from the Lord, but let it say to him, "Be Thou my helper; forsake me not, nor despise me, O God of my salvation."

Chapter 7. —Grace is Necessary Along with Free Will to Lead a Good Life.

Therefore, my dearly beloved, as we have now proved by our former testimonies from Holy Scripture that there is in man a free determination of will for living rightly and acting rightly; so now let us see what are the divine testimonies concerning the grace of God, without which we are not able to do any good thing. And first of all, I will say something about the very profession which you make in your brotherhood. Now your society, in which you are leading lives of continence, could not hold together unless you despised conjugal pleasure. Well, the Lord was one day conversing on this very topic, when His disciples remarked to Him, "If such be the case of a man with his wife, it is not good to marry." He then answered them, "All men cannot receive this saying, save they to whom it is given." And was it not to Timothy's free will that the apostle appealed, when he exhorted him in these words: "Keep thyself continent"? He also explained the power of the will in this matter when He said, "Having no necessity, but possessing power over his own will, to keep his virgin." And yet "all men do not receive this saying, except those to whom the power is given." Now they to whom this is not given either are unwilling or do not fulfil what they will; whereas they to whom it is given so will as to accomplish what they will. In order, therefore, that this saying, which is not received by all men, may yet be received by some, there are both the gift of God and free will.

Chapter 8. —Conjugal Chastity is Itself the Gift of God.

It is concerning conjugal chastity itself that the apostle treats, when he says, "Let him do what he will, he sinned not if he marry;" and yet this too is God's gift, for the Scripture says, "It is by the Lord that the woman is joined to her husband." Accordingly the teacher of the Gentiles, in one of his discourses, commends both conjugal chastity, whereby adulteries are prevented, and the still more perfect continence which foregoes all cohabitation, and shows how both one and the other are severally the gift of God. Writing to the Corinthians, he admonished married persons not to defraud each other; and then, after his admonition to these, he added: "But I could wish that all men were even as I am myself,"— meaning, of course, that he abstained from all cohabitation; and then proceeded to say: "But every man hath his own gift of God, one after this manner, and another after that." Now, do the many precepts which are written in the law of God, forbidding all fornication and adultery, indicate anything else than free will? Surely such precepts would not be given unless a man had a will of his own, wherewith to obey the divine commandments. And yet it is God's gift which is indispensable for the observance of the precepts of chastity. Accordingly, it is said in the Book of Wisdom: "When I knew that no one could be continent, except God gives it, then this became a point of wisdom to know whose gift it was." "Every man," however, "is tempted when he is drawn away of his own lust and enticed" not to observe and keep these holy precepts of chastity. If he should say in respect of these commandments, "I wish to keep them, but am mastered by my concupiscence," then the Scripture responds to his free will, as I have already said: "Be not overcome of evil but overcome evil with good." In order, however, that this victory may be gained, grace renders its help; and were not this help given, then the law would be nothing but the strength of sin. For concupiscence is increased and receives greater energies from the prohibition of the law, unless the spirit of grace helps. This explains the statement of the great Teacher of the Gentiles, when he says, "The sting of death is sin, and the strength of sin is the law." See, then, I pray you, whence originates this confession of weakness, when a man says, "I desire to keep what the law commands, but am overcome by the strength of my concupiscence." And when his will is addressed, and it is said, "Be not overcome of evil," of what avail is anything but the succor of God's grace to the accomplishment of the precept? This the apostle himself afterwards stated; for after saying "The strength of sin is the law," he immediately subjoined, "But thanks be to God, who giveth us the victory, through our Lord Jesus Christ." It follows, then, that the victory in which sin is vanquished is nothing else than the gift of God, who in this contest helps free will.

Chapter 9. —Entering into Temptation. Prayer is a Proof of Grace.

Wherefore, our Heavenly Master also says: "Watch and pray, that ye enter not into temptation." Let every man, therefore, when fighting against his own concupiscence, pray that he enter not into temptation; that is, that he be not drawn aside and enticed by it. But he does not enter into temptation if he conquers his evil concupiscence by good will. And yet the determination of the human will is insufficient, unless the Lord grant it victory in answer to prayer that it enter not into temptation. What, indeed, affords clearer evidence of the grace of God than the acceptance of prayer in any petition? If our Savior had only said, "Watch that ye enter not into temptation," He would appear to have done nothing further than admonish man's will; but since He added the words, "and pray," He showed that God helps us not to enter into temptation. It is to the free will of man that the words are addressed: "My son, remove not thyself from the chastening of the Lord." And the Lord said: "I have prayed for thee, Peter, that thy faith fail not." So that a man is assisted by grace, in order that his will may not be uselessly commanded.

Chapter 10 [V.]—Free Will and God's Grace are Simultaneously Commended.

When God says, "Turn ye unto me, and I will turn unto you," one of these clauses—that which invites our return to God—evidently belongs to our will; while the other, which promises His return to us, belongs to His grace. Here, possibly, the Pelagians think they have a justification for their opinion which they so prominently advance, that God's grace is given according to our merits. In the East, indeed, that is to say, in the province of Palestine, in which is the city of Jerusalem, Pelagius, when examined in person by the bishop, did not venture to affirm this. For it happened that among the objections which were brought up against him, this in particular was objected, that he maintained that the grace of God was given according to our merits,—an opinion which was so diverse from catholic doctrine, and so hostile to the grace of Christ, that unless he had anathematized it, as laid to his charge, he himself must have been anathematized on its account. He pronounced, indeed, the required anathema upon the dogma, but how insincerely his later books plainly show; for in them he maintains absolutely no other opinion than that the grace of God is given according to our merits. Such passages do they collect out of the Scriptures, —like the one which I just now quoted, "Turn ye unto me, and I will turn unto you,"—as if it were owing to the merit of our turning to God that His grace were given us, wherein He Himself even turns unto us. Now the persons who hold this opinion fail to observe that, unless our turning to God were itself God's gift, it would not be said to Him in prayer, "Turn us again, O God of hosts;" and, "Thou, O God, wilt turn and quicken us;" and again, "Turn us, O God of our salvation,"—with other passages of similar import, too numerous to mention here. For, with respect to our coming unto Christ, what else does it mean than our being turned to Him by believing? And yet He says: "No man can come unto me, except it were given unto him of my Father."

Chapter 11. —Other Passages of Scripture Which the Pelagians Abuse.

Then, again, there is the Scripture contained in the second book of the Chronicles: "The Lord is with you when ye are with Him: and if ye shall seek Him ye shall find Him; but if ye forsake Him, He also will forsake you." This passage, no doubt, clearly manifests the choice of the will. But they who maintain that God's grace is given according to our merits, receive these testimonies of

Scripture in such a manner as to believe that our merit lies in the circumstance of our "being with God," while His grace is given according to this merit, so that He too may be with us. In like manner, that our merit lies in the fact of "our seeking God," and then His grace is given according to this merit, in order that we may find Him." Again, there is a passage in the first book of the same Chronicles which declares the choice of the will: "And thou, Solomon, my son, know thou the God of thy father, and serve Him with a perfect heart and with a willing mind, for the Lord searched all hearts, and understand all the imaginations of the thoughts; if thou seek Him, He will be found of thee; but if thou forsake Him, He will cast thee off forever." But these people find some room for human merit in the clause, "If thou seek Him," and then the grace is thought to be given according to this merit in what is said in the ensuing words, "He will be found of thee." And so they labor with all their might to show that God's grace is given according to our merits, —in other words, that grace is not grace. For, as the apostle most expressly says, to them who receive reward according to merit "the recompense is not reckoned of grace but of debt."

Chapter 12. —He Proves Out of St. Paul that Grace is Not Given According to Men's Merits.

Now there was, no doubt, a decided merit in the Apostle Paul, but it was an evil one, while he persecuted the Church, and he says of it: "I am not meet to be called an apostle, because I persecuted the Church of God." And it was while he had this evil merit that a good one was rendered to him instead of the evil; and, therefore, he went on at once to say, "But by the grace of God I am what I am." Then, in order to exhibit also his free will, he added in the next clause, "And His grace within me was not in vain, but I have labored more abundantly than they all." This free will of man he appeals to in the case of others also, as when he says to them, "We beseech you that ye receive not the grace of God in vain." Now, how could he so enjoin them, if they received God's grace in such a manner as to lose their own will? Nevertheless, lest the will itself should be deemed capable of doing any good thing without the grace of God, after saying, "His grace within me was not in vain, but I have labored more abundantly than they all," he immediately added the qualifying clause, "Yet not I, but the grace of God which was with me." In other words, Not I alone, but the grace of God with me. And thus, neither was it the grace of God alone, nor was it he himself alone, but it was the grace of God with him. For his call, however, from heaven and his conversion by that great and most effectual call, God's grace was alone, because his merits, though great, were yet evil. Then, to quote one passage more, he says to Timothy: "But be thou a co-laborer with the gospel, according to the power of God, who saves us and called us with His holy calling, —not according to our works but according to His own purpose and grace, which was given us in Christ Jesus." Then, elsewhere, he enumerates his merits, and gives us this description of their evil character: "For we ourselves also were formerly foolish, unbelieving, deceived, serving divers lusts and pleasures, living in malice and envy, hateful, and hating one another." Nothing, to be sure, but punishment was due to such a course of evil desert! God, however, who returns good for evil by His grace, which is not given according to our merits, enabled the apostle to conclude his statement and say: "But when the kindness and love of our Savior God shone upon us,—not of works of righteousness which we have done, but according to His mercy He saved us, by the laver of regeneration and renewal of the Holy Ghost, whom He shed upon us abundantly through Jesus Christ our Savior; that, being justified by His grace, we should be made heirs according to the hope of eternal life."

Chapter 13 [VI.]—The Grace of God is Not Given According to Merit, But Itself Makes All Good Desert.

From these and similar passages of Scripture, we gather the proof that God's grace is not given according to our merits. The truth is, we see that it is given not only where there are no good, but even where there are many evil merits preceding: and we see it so given daily. But it is plain that when it has been given, also our good merits begin to be, —yet only by means of it; for, were that only to withdraw itself, man falls, not raised up, but precipitated by free will. Wherefore no man ought, even when he begins to possess good merits, to attribute them to himself, but to God, who is thus addressed by the Psalmist: "Be Thou my helper, forsake me not." By saying, "Forsake me not," he shows that if he were to be forsaken, he is unable of himself to do any good thing. Wherefore also he says: "I said in my abundance, I shall never be moved," for he thought that he had such an abundance of good to call his own that he would not be moved. But in order that he might be taught whose that was, of which he had begun to boast as if it were his own, he was admonished by the gradual desertion of God's grace, and says: "O Lord, in Thy good pleasure Thou didst add strength to my beauty. Thou didst, however, turn away Thy face, and then I was troubled and distressed." Thus, it is necessary for a man that he should be not only justified when unrighteous by the grace of God,—that is, be changed from unholiness to righteousness,—when he is requited with good for his evil; but that, even after he has become justified by faith, grace should accompany him on his way, and he should lean upon it, lest he fall. On this account it is written concerning the Church herself in the book of Canticles: "Who is this that cometh up in white raiment, leaning upon her kinsman?" Made white is she who by herself alone could not be white. And by whom has she been made white except by Him who says by the prophet, "Though your sins be as purple, I will make them white as snow"? At the time, then, that she was made white, she deserved nothing good; but now that she is made white, she walks well; —but it is only by her continuing ever to lean upon Him by whom she was made white. Wherefore, Jesus Himself, on whom she leans that was made white, said to His disciples, "Without me ye can do nothing."

Chapter 14. —Paul First Received Grace that He Might Win the Crown.

Let us return now to the Apostle Paul, who, as we have found, obtained God's grace, who recompenses good for evil, without any good merits of his own, but rather with many evil merits. Let us see what he says when his final sufferings were approaching, writing to Timothy: "I am now ready to be offered, and the time of my departure is at hand. I have fought a good fight; I have finished my course; I have kept the faith." He enumerates these as, of course, now his good merits; so that, as after his evil merits he obtained grace, so now, after his good merits, he might receive the crown. Observe, therefore, what follows: "There is henceforth laid up for me," he says, "a crown of righteousness, which the Lord, the righteous Judge, shall give me at that day." Now, to whom should the righteous Judge award the crown, except to him on whom the merciful Father had bestowed grace? And how could the crown be one "of righteousness," unless the grace had preceded which "justified the ungodly"? How, moreover, could these things now be awarded as of debt, unless the other had been before given as a free gift?

Chapter 15. —The Pelagians Profess that the Only Grace Which is Not Given According to Our Merits is that of the Forgiveness of Sins.

When, however, the Pelagians say that the only grace which is not given according to our merits is that whereby his sins are forgiven to man, but that that which is given in the end, that is, eternal life, is rendered to our preceding merits: they must not be allowed to go without an answer. If, indeed, they so understand our merits as to acknowledge them, too, to be the gifts of God, then their opinion would not deserve reprobation. But since they so preach human merits as to declare that a man has them of his own self, then most rightly the apostle replies: "Who makes thee to differ from another? And what hast thou, that thou didst not receive? Now, if you did receive it, why do you glory as if you had not received it?" To a man who holds such views, it is perfect truth to say: It is His own gifts that God crowns, not your merits, —if, at least, your merits are of your own self, not of Him. If, indeed, they are such, they are evil; and God does not crown them; but if they are good, they are God's gifts, because, as the Apostle James says, "Every good gift and every perfect gift is from above, and cometh down from the Father of lights." In accordance with which John also, the Lord's forerunner, declares: "A man can receive nothing except it be given him from heaven"—from heaven, of course, because from thence came also the Holy Ghost, when Jesus ascended up on high, led captivity captive, and gave gifts to men. If, then, your good merits are God's gifts, God does not crown your merits as your merits, but as His own gifts.

Chapter 16 [VII.]—Paul Fought, But God Gave the Victory: He Ran, But God Showed Mercy.

Let us, therefore, consider those very merits of the Apostle Paul which he said the Righteous Judge would recompense with the crown of righteousness; and let us see whether these merits of his were really his own—I mean, whether they were obtained by him of himself, or were the gifts of God. "I have fought," says he, "the good fight; I have finished my course; I have kept the faith." Now, in the first place, these good works were nothing, unless they had been preceded by good thoughts. Observe, therefore, what he says concerning these very thoughts. His words, when writing to the Corinthians, are: "Not that we are sufficient of ourselves to think anything as of ourselves; but our sufficiency is of God." Then let us look at each several merit. "I have fought the good fight." Well, now, I want to know by what power he fought. Was it by a power which he possessed of himself, or by strength given to him from above? It is impossible to suppose that so great a teacher as the apostle was ignorant of the law of God, which proclaims the following in Deuteronomy: "Say not in thine heart, My own strength and energy of hand hath wrought for me this great power; but thou shalt remember the Lord thy God, how it is He that giveth thee strength to acquire such power." And what avails "the good fight," unless followed by victory? And who gives the victory but He of whom the apostle says himself, "Thanks be to God, who giveth us the victory through our Lord Jesus Christ"? Then, in another passage, having quoted from the Psalm these words: "Because for Thy sake we are killed all the day long; we are accounted as sheep for slaughter," he went on to declare: "Nay, in all these things we are more than conquerors, through Him that loved us." Not by ourselves, therefore, is the victory accomplished, but by Him who hath loved us. In the second clause he says, "I have finished my course." Now, who is it that says this, but he who declares in another passage, "So then it is not of him that wills, nor of him that runs, but of God that shows mercy." And this sentence can by no means be transposed, so that it could be said: It is not of God, who shows mercy, but of the man who wills and runs. If any person be bold enough to express the matter thus, he shows himself most plainly to be at issue with the apostle.

Chapter 17. —The Faith that He Kept Was the Free Gift of God.

His last clause runs thus: "I have kept the faith." But he who says this is the same who declares in another passage, "I have obtained mercy that I might be faithful."

He does not say, "I obtained mercy because I was faithful," but "in order that I might be faithful," thus showing that even faith itself cannot be had without God's mercy, and that it is the gift of God. This he very expressly teaches us when he says, "For by grace are ye saved through faith, and that not of yourselves; it is the gift of God." They might possibly say, "We received grace because we believed;" as if they would attribute the faith to themselves, and the grace to God. Therefore, the apostle having said, "Ye are saved through faith," added," And that not of yourselves, but it is the gift of God." And again, lest they should say they deserved so great a gift by their works, he immediately added, "Not of works, lest any man should boast." Not that he denied good works, or emptied them of their value, when he says that God renders to every man according to his works; but because works proceed from faith, and not faith from works. Therefore, it is from Him that we have works of righteousness, from whom comes also faith itself, concerning which it is written, "The just shall live by faith."

Chapter 18. —Faith Without Good Works is Not Sufficient for Salvation.

Unintelligent persons, however, about the apostle's statement: "We conclude that a man is justified by faith without the works of the law," have thought him to mean that faith suffices to a man, even if he leads a bad life, and has no good works. Impossible is it that such a character should be deemed "a vessel of election" by the apostle, who, after declaring that "in Christ Jesus neither circumcision availed anything, nor uncircumcision," adds at once, "but faith which worketh by love." It is such faith which severs God's faithful from unclean demons, —for even these "believe and tremble," as the Apostle James says; but they do not do well. Therefore, they possess not the faith by which the just man lives, —the faith which works by love in such wise, that God recompenses it according to its works with eternal life. But since we have even our good works from God, from whom likewise comes our faith and our love, therefore the selfsame great teacher of the Gentiles has designated "eternal life" itself as His gracious "gift."

Chapter 19 [VIII.]—How is Eternal Life Both a Reward for Service and a Free Gift of Grace?

And hence there arises no small question, which must be solved by the Lord's gift. If eternal life is rendered to good works, as the Scripture most openly declares: "Then He shall reward every man according to his works:" how can eternal life be a matter of grace, seeing that grace is not rendered to works, but is given gratuitously, as the apostle himself tells us: "To him that worketh is the reward not reckoned of grace, but of debt;" and again: "There is a remnant saved according to the election of grace;" with these words immediately subjoined: "And if of grace, then is it no more of works; otherwise grace is no more grace"? How, then, is eternal life by grace, when it is received from works? Does the apostle perchance not say that eternal life is a grace? Nay, he has so called it, with a clearness which none can possibly gainsay. It requires no acute intellect, but only an attentive reader, to discover this. For after saying, "The wages of sin is death," he at once added, "The grace of

God is eternal life through Jesus Christ our Lord."

Chapter 20. —The Question Answered. Justification is Grace Simply and Entirely, Eternal Life is Reward and Grace.

This question, then, seems to me to be by no means capable of solution, unless we understand that even those good works of ours, which are recompensed with eternal life, belong to the grace of God, because of what is said by the Lord Jesus: "Without me ye can do nothing." And the apostle himself, after saying, "By grace are ye saved through faith; and that not of yourselves, it is the gift of God: not of works, lest any man should boast;" saw, of course, the possibility that men would think from this statement that good works are not necessary to those who believe, but that faith alone suffices for them; and again, the possibility of men's boasting of their good works, as if they were of themselves capable of performing them. To meet, therefore, these opinions on both sides, he immediately added, "For we are His workmanship, created in Christ Jesus unto good works, which God hath before ordained that we should walk in them." What is the purport of his saying, "Not of works, lest any man should boast," while commending the grace of God? And then why does he afterwards, when giving a reason for using such words, say, "For we are His workmanship, created in Christ Jesus unto good works"? Why, therefore, does it run, "Not of works, lest any man should boast"? Now, hear and understand. "Not of works" is spoken of the works which you suppose have their origin in yourself alone; but you must think of works for which God has molded (that is, has formed and created) you. For of these he says, "We are His workmanship, created in Christ Jesus unto good works." Now he does not here speak of that creation which made us human beings, but of that in reference to which one said who was already in full manhood, "Create in me a clean heart, O God;" concerning which also the apostle says, "Therefore, if any man be in Christ, he is a new creature: old things are passed away; behold, all things are become new. And all things are of God." We are framed, therefore, that is, formed and created, "in the good works which" we have not ourselves prepared, but "God hath before ordained that we should walk in them." It follows, then, dearly beloved, beyond all doubt, that as your good life is nothing else than God's grace, so also the eternal life which is the recompense of a good life is the grace of God; moreover it is given gratuitously, even as that is given gratuitously to which it is given. But that to which it is given is solely and simply grace; this therefore is also that which is given to it, because it is its reward; —grace is for grace, as if remuneration for righteousness; in order that it may be true, because it is true, that God "shall reward every man according to his works."

Chapter 21 [IX.]—Eternal Life is "Grace for Grace."

Perhaps you ask whether we ever read in the Sacred Scriptures of "grace for grace." Well you possess the Gospel according to John, which is perfectly clear in its very great light. Here John the Baptist says of Christ: "Of His fulness have we all received, even grace for grace." So that out of His fulness we have received, according to our humble measure, our particles of ability as it were for leading good lives— "according as God hath dealt to every man his measure of faith;" because "every man hath his proper gift of God; one after this manner, and another after that." And this is grace. But, over and above this, we shall also receive "grace for grace," when we shall have awarded to us eternal life, of which the apostle said: "The grace of God is eternal life through Jesus Christ our Lord," having just said that "the wages of sin is death." Deservedly did he call it "wages," because everlasting death is awarded as its proper due to diabolical service. Now, when it was in his power to say, and rightly to say: "But the wages of righteousness is eternal life," he yet preferred to say: "The grace of God is eternal life;" in order that we may hence understand that God does not, for any merits of our own, but from His own divine compassion, prolong our existence to everlasting life. Even as the Psalmist says to his soul, "Who crowned thee with mercy and compassion." Well, now, is not a crown given as the reward of good deeds? It is, however, only because He works good works in good men, of whom it is said, "It is God which worketh in you both to will and to do of His good pleasure," that the Psalm has it, as just now quoted: "He crowned thee with mercy and compassion," since it is through His mercy that we perform the good deeds to which the crown is awarded. It is not, however, to be for a moment supposed, because he said, "It is God that worketh in you both to will and to do of his own good pleasure," that free will is taken away. If this, indeed, had been his meaning, he would not have said just before, "Work out your own salvation with fear and trembling." For when the command is given "to work," their free will is addressed; and when it is added, "with fear and trembling," they are warned against boasting of their good deeds as if they were their own, by attributing to themselves the performance of anything good. It is pretty much as if the apostle had this question put to him: "Why did you use the phrase, 'with fear and trembling'?" And as if he answered the inquiry of his examiners by telling them, "For it is God which worketh in you." Because if you fear and tremble, you do not boast of your good works—as if they were your own, since it is God who works within you.

Chapter 22 [X.]—Who is the Transgressor of the Law? The Oldness of Its Letter. The Newness of Its Spirit.

Therefore, brethren, you ought by free will not do evil but do good; this, indeed, is the lesson taught us in the law of God, in the Holy Scriptures—both Old and New. Let us, however, read, and by the Lord's help understand, what the apostle tells us: "Because by the deeds of the law there shall no flesh be justified in His sight; for by the law is the knowledge of sin." Observe, he says "the knowledge," not "the destruction," of sin. But when a man knows sin, and grace does not help him to avoid what he knows, undoubtedly the law works wrath. And this the apostle explicitly says in another passage. His words are: "The law worketh wrath." The reason of this statement lies in the fact that God's wrath is greater in the case of the transgressor who by the law knows sin, and yet commits it; such a man is thus a transgressor of the law, even as the apostle says in another sentence, "For where no law is, there is no transgression." It is in accordance with this principle that he elsewhere says,

"That we may serve in newness of spirit, and not in the oldness of the letter;" wishing the law to be here understood by "the oldness of the letter," and what else by "newness of spirit" than grace? Then, that it might not be thought that he had brought any accusation, or suggested any blame, against the law, he immediately takes himself to task with this inquiry: "What shall we say, then? Is the law sin? God forbid." He then adds the statement: "Nay, I had not known sin but by the law;" which is of the same import as the passage above quoted: "By the law is the knowledge of sin." Then: "For I had not known lust," he says, "except the law had said, 'Thou shalt not covet.' But sin, taking occasion by the commandment, wrought in me all manner of concupiscence. For without the law sin was dead. For I was alive without the law once; but when the commandment came, sin revived, and I died. And the commandment, which was ordained to life, I found to be unto death. For sin, taking occasion by the commandment, deceived me, and by it slew me. Wherefore the law is holy; and the commandment holy, just, and good. Was, then, that which is good made death unto me? God forbid. But sin, that it might appear sin, worked death in me by that which is good, —in order that the sinner, or the sin, might by the commandment become beyond measure." And to the Galatians he writes: "Knowing that a man is not justified by the works of the law, except through faith in Jesus Christ, even we have believed in Jesus Christ, that we might be justified by the faith of Christ, and not by the works of the law; for by the works of the law shall no flesh be justified."

Chapter 23 [XI.]—The Pelagians Maintain that the Law is the Grace of God Which Helps Us Not to Sin.

Why, therefore, do those very vain and perverse Pelagians say that the law is the grace of God by which we are helped not to sin? Do they not, by making such an allegation, unhappily and beyond all doubt contradict the great apostle? He, indeed, says, that by the law sin received strength against man; and that man, by the commandment, although it be holy, and just, and good, nevertheless dies, and that death works in him through that which is good, from which death there is no deliverance unless the Spirit quickens him, whom the letter had killed,—as he says in another passage, "The letter kills, but the Spirit gives life." And yet these obstinate persons, blind to God's light, and deaf to His voice, maintain that the letter which kills gives life, and thus gainsay the quickening Spirit. "Therefore, brethren" (that I may warn you with better effect in the words of the apostle himself), "we are debtors not to the flesh, to live after the flesh; for if ye live after the flesh ye shall die; but if ye through the Spirit do mortify the deeds of the body, ye shall live." I have said this to deter your free will from evil, and to exhort it to good by apostolic words; but yet you must not therefore glory in man,—that is to say, in your own selves,—and not in the Lord, when you live not after the flesh, but through the Spirit mortify the deeds of the flesh. For in order that they to whom the apostle addressed this language might not exalt themselves, thinking that they were themselves able of their own spirit to do such good works as these, and not by the Spirit of God, after saying to them, "If ye through the Spirit do mortify the deeds of the flesh, ye shall live," he at once added, "For as many as are led by the Spirit of God, they are the sons of God." When, therefore, you by the Spirit mortify the deeds of the flesh, that you may have life, glorify Him, praise Him, give thanks to Him by whose Spirit you are so led as to be able to do such things as show you to be the children of God; "for as many as are led by the Spirit of God, they are the sons of God."

Chapter 24 [XII.]—Who May Be Said to Wish to Establish Their Own Righteousness. "God's Righteousness," So Called, Which Man Has from God.

As many, therefore, as are led by their own spirit, trusting in their own virtue, with the addition merely of the law's assistance, without the help of grace, are not the sons of God. Such are they of whom the same apostle speaks as "being ignorant of God's righteousness, and wishing to establish their own righteousness, who have not submitted themselves to the righteousness of God." He said this of the Jews, who in their self-assumption rejected grace, and therefore did not believe in Christ. Their own righteousness, indeed, he says, they wish to establish; and this righteousness is of the law,—not that the law was established by themselves, but that they had constituted their righteousness in the law which is of God, when they supposed themselves able to fulfil that law by their own strength, ignorant of God's righteousness,—not indeed that by which God is Himself righteous, but that which man has from God. And that you may know that he designated as theirs the righteousness which is of the law, and as God's that which man receives from God, hear what he says in another passage, when speaking of Christ: "For whose sake I counted all things not only as loss, but

I deemed them to be dung, that I might win Christ, and be found in Him—not having my own righteousness, which is of the law, but that which is through the faith of Christ, which is of God." Now what does he mean by "not having my own righteousness, which is of the law," when the law is really not his at all, but God's,—except this, that he called it his own righteousness, although it was of the law, because he thought he could fulfil the law by his own will, without the aid of grace which is through faith in Christ? Wherefore, after saying, "Not having my own righteousness, which is of the law," he immediately subjoined, "But that which is through the faith of Christ, which is of God." This is what they were ignorant of, of whom he says, "Being ignorant of God's righteousness,"—that is, the righteousness which is of God (for it is given not by the letter, which kills, but by the life-giving Spirit), "and wishing to establish their own righteousness," which he expressly described as the righteousness of the law, when he said, "Not having my own righteousness, which is of the law;" they were not subject to the righteousness of God,—in other words, they submitted not themselves to the grace of God. For they were under the law, not under grace, and therefore sin had dominion over them, from which a man is not freed by the law, but by grace. On which account he elsewhere says, "For sin shall not have dominion over you; because ye are not under the law, but under grace." Not that the law is evil; but because they are under its power, whom it makes guilty by imposing commandments, not by aiding. It is by grace that any one is a doer of the law; and without this grace, he who is placed under the law will be only a hearer of the law. To such persons he addresses these words: "Ye who are justified by the law are fallen from grace."

Chapter 25 [XIII.]—As The Law is Not, So Neither is Our Nature Itself that Grace by Which We are Christians.

Now who can be so insensible to the words of the apostle, who so foolishly, nay, so insanely ignorant of the purport of his statement, as to venture to affirm that the law is grace, when he who knew very well what he was saying emphatically declares, "Ye who are justified by the law are fallen from grace"? Well, but if the law is not grace, seeing that in order that the law itself may be kept, it is not the law, but only grace which can give help, will not nature at any rate be grace? For this, too, the Pelagians have been bold enough to aver, that grace is the nature in which we were created, so as to possess a rational mind, by which we are enabled to understand,— formed as we are in the image of God, so as to have dominion over the fish of the sea, and over the fowl of the air, and over every living thing that crept upon the earth. This, however, is not the grace which the apostle commends to us through the faith of Jesus Christ. For it is certain that we possess this nature in common with ungodly men and unbelievers; whereas the grace which comes through the faith of Jesus Christ belongs only to them to whom the faith itself appertains. "For all men have not faith." Now, as the apostle, with perfect truth, says to those who by wishing to be justified by the law have fallen from grace, "If righteousness come by the law, then Christ is dead in vain;" so likewise, to those who think that the grace which he commends and faith in Christ receives, is nature, the same language is with the same degree of truth applicable: if righteousness come from nature, then Christ is dead in vain. But the law was in existence up to that time, and it did not justify; and nature existed too, but it did not justify. It was not, then, in vain that Christ died, in order that the law might be fulfilled through Him who said, "I am come not to destroy the law, but to fulfil it;" and that our nature, which was lost through Adam, might through Him be recovered, who said that "He was come to seek and to save that which was lost;" in whose coming the old fathers likewise who loved God believed.

Chapter 26. —The Pelagians Contend that the Grace, Which is Neither the Law Nor Nature, Avails Only to the Remission of Past Sins, But Not to the Avoidance of Future Ones.

They also maintain that God's grace, which is given through the faith of Jesus Christ, and which is neither the law nor nature, avails only for the remission of sins that have been committed, and not for the shunning of future ones, or the subjugation of those which are now assailing us. Now if all this were true, surely after offering the petition of the Lord's Prayer, "Forgive us our debts, as we forgive our debtors," we could hardly go on and say, "And lead us not into temptation." The former petition we present that our sins may be forgiven; the latter, that they may be avoided or subdued, —a favor which we should by no means beg of our Father who is in heaven if we were able to accomplish it by the virtue of our human will. Now I strongly advise and earnestly require your Love to read attentively the book of the blessed Cyprian which he wrote On the Lord's Prayer. As far as the Lord shall assist you, understand it, and commit it to memory. In this work you will see how he so appeals to the free will of those whom he edifies in his treatise, as to show them, that whatever they must fulfil in the law, they must ask for in the prayer. But this, of course, would be utterly empty if the human will were sufficient for the performance without the help of God.

Chapter 27 [XIV.]—Grace Effects the Fulfilment of the Law, the Deliverance of Nature, and the Suppression of Sin's Dominion.

It has, however, been shown to demonstration that instead of really maintaining free will, they have only inflated a theory of it, which, having no stability, has fallen to the ground. Neither the knowledge of God's law, nor nature, nor the mere remission of sins is that grace which is given to us through our Lord Jesus Christ; but it is this very grace which accomplishes the fulfilment of the law, and the liberation of nature, and the removal of the dominion of sin. Being, therefore, convicted on these points, they resort to another expedient, and endeavor to show in some way or other that the grace of God is given us according to our merits. For they say: "Granted that it is not given to us according to the merits of good works, inasmuch as it is through it that we do any good thing, still it is given to us according to the merits of a good will; for," say they, "the good will of him who prays precedes his prayer, even as the will of the believer preceded his faith, so that according to these merits the grace of God who hears, follows."

Chapter 28. —Faith is the Gift of God.

I have already discussed the point concerning faith, that is, concerning the will of him who believes, even so far as to show that it appertains to grace,—so that the apostle did not tell us, "I have obtained mercy because I was faithful;" but he said, "I have obtained mercy in order to be faithful." And there are many other passages of similar import,—among them that in which he bids us "think soberly, according as God hath dealt out to every man the proportion of faith;" and that which I have already quoted: "By grace are ye saved through faith; and that not of yourselves; it is the gift of God;" and again another in the same Epistle to the Ephesians: "Peace be to the brethren, and love with faith, from God the Father, and the Lord Jesus Christ;" and to the same effect that passage in which he says, "For unto you it is given in the behalf of Christ not only to believe on Him, but also to suffer for His sake." Both alike are therefore due to the grace of God, —the faith of those who believe, and the patience of those who suffer, because the apostle spoke of both as given. Then, again, there is the passage, especially noticeable, in which he says, "We, having the same spirit of faith," for his phrase is not "the knowledge of faith," but "the spirit of faith;" and he expressed himself thus in order that we might understand how that faith is given to us, even when it is not sought, so that other blessings may be granted to it at its request. For "how," says he, "shall they call upon Him in whom they have not believed?" The spirit of grace, therefore, causes us to have faith, in order that through faith we may, on praying for it, obtain the ability to do what we are commanded. On this account the apostle himself constantly puts faith before the law;

since we are not able to do what the law commands unless we obtain the strength to do it by the prayer of faith.

Chapter 29. —God is Able to Convert Opposing Wills, and to Take Away from the Heart Its Hardness.

Now if faith is simply of free will, and is not given by God, why do we pray for those who will not believe, that they may believe? This it would be absolutely useless to do, unless we believe, with perfect propriety, that Almighty God is able to turn to belief wills that are perverse and opposed to faith. Man's free will is addressed when it is said, "Today, if ye will hear His voice, harden not your hearts." But if God were not able to remove from the human heart even its obstinacy and hardness, He would not say, through the prophet, "I will take from them their heart of stone and will give them a heart of flesh." That all this was foretold about the New Testament is shown clearly enough by the apostle when he says, "Ye are our epistle, . . . written not with ink, but with the Spirit of the living God; not in tables of stone, but in fleshly tables of the heart." We must not, of course, suppose that such a phrase as this is used as if those might live in a fleshly way who ought to live spiritually; but since a stone has no feeling, with which man's hard heart is compared, what was there left Him to compare man's intelligent heart with but the flesh, which possesses feeling? For this is what is said by the prophet Ezekiel: "I will give them another heart, and I will put a new spirit within you; and I will take the stony heart out of their flesh, and will give them a heart of flesh; that they may walk in my statutes, and keep mine ordinances, and do them: and they shall be my people, and I will be their

God, says the Lord." Now can we possibly, without extreme absurdity, maintain that there previously existed in any man the good merit of a good will, to entitle him to the removal of his stony heart, when all the while this very heart of stone signifies nothing else than a will of the hardest kind and such as is absolutely inflexible against God? For where a good will precedes, there is, of course, no longer a heart of stone.

Chapter 30. —The Grace by Which the Stony Heart is Removed is Not Preceded by Good Deserts, But by Evil Ones.

In another passage, also, by the same prophet, God, in the clearest language, shows us that it is not owing to any good merits on the part of men, but for His own name's sake, that He does these things. This is His language: "This I do, O house of Israel, but for mine holy name's sake, which ye have profaned among the heathen, whither ye went. And I will sanctify my great name, which was profaned among the heathen, which ye have profaned in the midst of them; and the heathen shall know that I am the Lord, says the Lord God, when I shall be sanctified in you before their eyes. For I will take you from among the heathen, and gather you out of all countries, and will bring you into your own land. Then will I sprinkle you with clean water, and ye shall be clean: from all your own filthiness, and from all your idols will I cleanse you. A new heart also will I give you, and a new spirit will I put within you; and the stony heart shall be taken away out of your flesh, and I will give you a heart of flesh. And I will put my Spirit within you, and will cause you to walk in my statutes, and ye shall keep my judgments, and do them." Now who is so blind as not to see, and who so stone-like as not to feel, that this grace is not given according to the merits of a good will, when the Lord declares and testifies, "It is I, O house of Israel, who do this, but for my holy name's sake"? Now why did He say, "It is I that do it, but for my holy name's sake," were it not that they should not think that it was owing to their own good merits that these things were happening, as the Pelagians hesitate not unblushingly to say? But there were not only no good merits of theirs, but the Lord shows that evil ones actually preceded; for He says, "But for my holy name's sake, which ye have profaned among the heathen." Who can fail to observe how dreadful is the evil of profaning the Lord's own holy name? And yet, for the sake of this very name of mine, says He, which ye have profaned, I, even I, will make you good, but not for your own sakes; and, as He adds, "I will sanctify my great name, which was profaned among the heathen, which ye have profaned in the midst of them." He says that He sanctifies His name, which He had already declared to be holy. Therefore, this is just what we pray for in the Lord's Prayer— "Hallowed be Thy name." We ask for the hallowing among men of that which is in itself undoubtedly always holy. Then it follows, "And the heathen shall know that I am the Lord, says the Lord God, when I shall be sanctified in you." Although, then, He is Himself always holy, He is, nevertheless, sanctified in those on whom He bestows His grace, by taking from them that stony heart by which they profaned the name of the Lord.

Chapter 31 [XV.]—Free Will Has Its Function in the Heart's Conversion; But Grace Too Has Its.

Lest, however, it should be thought that men themselves in this matter do nothing by free will, it is said in the Psalm, "Harden not your hearts;" and in Ezekiel himself, "Cast away from you all your transgressions, which ye have impiously committed against me; and make you a new heart and a new spirit; and keep all my commandments. For why will ye die, O house of Israel, says the Lord? for I have no pleasure in the death of him that dies, says the Lord God: and turn ye, and live." We should remember that it is He who says, "Turn ye and live," to whom it is said in prayer, "Turn us again, O God." We should remember that He says, "Cast away from you all your transgressions," when it is even He who justifies the ungodly. We should remember that He says, "Make you a new heart and a new spirit," who also promises, "I will give you a new heart, and a new spirit will I put within you." How is it, then, that He who says, "Make you," also says, "I will give you"? Why does He command, if He is to give? Why does He give if man is to make, except it be that He gives what He commands when He helps him to obey whom He commands? There is, however, always within us a free will, —but it is not always good; for it is either free from righteousness when it serves sin, —and then it is evil, —or else it is free from sin when it serves righteousness, —and then it is good. But the grace of God is always good; and by it it comes to pass that a man is of a good will, though he was before of an evil one. By it also it comes to pass that the very good will, which has now begun to be, is enlarged, and made so great that it is able to fulfil the divine commandments which it shall wish, when it shall once firmly and perfectly wish. This is the purport of what the Scripture says: "If thou wilt, thou shalt keep the commandments;" so that the man who wills but is not able knows that he does not yet fully will, and prays that he may have so great a will that it may suffice for keeping the commandments. And thus, indeed, he receives assistance to perform what he is commanded. Then is the will of use when we have ability; just as ability is also then of use when we have the will. For what does it profit us if we will what we are unable to do, or else do not will what we are able to do?

Chapter 32 [XVI.]—In What Sense It is Rightly Said That, If We Like, We May Keep God's Commandments.

The Pelagians think that they know something great when they assert that "God would not command what He knew could not be done by man." Who can be ignorant of this? But God commands some things which we cannot do, in order that we may know what we ought to ask of Him. For this is faith itself, which obtains by prayer what the law commands. He, indeed, who said, "If thou wilt, thou shalt keep the commandments," did in the same book of Ecclesiasticus afterwards say, "Who shall give a watch before my mouth, and a seal of wisdom upon my lips, that I fall not suddenly thereby, and that my tongue destroys me not." Now he had certainly heard and received these commandments: "Keep thy tongue from evil, and thy lips from speaking guile." Forasmuch, then, as what he said is true: "If thou wilt, thou shalt keep the commandments," why does he want a watch to be given before his mouth, like him who says in the Psalm, "Set a watch, O Lord, before my mouth"? Why is he not satisfied with God's commandment and his own will; since, if he has the will, he shall keep the commandments? How many of God's commandments are directed against pride! He is quite aware of them; if he will, he may keep them. Why, therefore, does he shortly afterwards say, "O God, Father and God of my life, give me not a proud look"? The law had long ago said to him, "Thou shalt not covet;" let him then only will, and do what he is bidden, because, if he has the will, he shall keep the commandments. Why, therefore, does he afterwards say, "Turn away from me concupiscence"? Against luxury, too, how many commandments has God enjoined! Let a man observe them; because, if he will, he may keep the commandments. But what means that cry to God, "Let not the greediness of the belly nor lust of the flesh take hold on me!"? Now, if we were to put this question to him personally, he would very rightly answer us and say, From that prayer of mine, in which I offer this particular petition to God, you may understand in what sense I said, "If thou wilt, thou mayest keep the commandments." For it is certain that we keep the commandments if we will; but because the will is prepared by the Lord, we must ask of Him for such a force of will as suffices to make us act by the willing. It is certain that it is we that will when we will, but it is He who makes us will what is good, of whom it is said (as he has just now expressed it), "The will is prepared by the Lord." Of the same Lord it is said, "The steps of a man are ordered by the Lord, and his way doth He will." Of the same Lord again it is said, "It is God who worketh in you, even to will!" It is certain that it is we that act when we act; but it is He who makes us act, by applying efficacious powers to our will, who has said, "I will make you to walk in my statutes, and to observe my judgments, and to do them." When he says, "I will make you . . . to do them," what else does He say in fact than, "I will take away from you your heart of stone," from which used to arise your inability to act, "and I will give you a heart of flesh," in order that you may act? And what does this promise amount to but this: I will remove your hard heart, out of which you did not act, and I will give you an obedient heart, out of which you shall act? It is He who causes us to act, to whom the human suppliant says, "Set a watch, O Lord, before my mouth." That is to say: Make or enable me, O Lord, to set a watch before my mouth, — a benefit which he had already obtained from God who thus described its influence: "I set a watch upon my mouth."

Chapter 33 [XVII.]—A Good Will May Be Small and Weak; An Ample Will, Great Love. Operating and Co-operating Grace.

He, therefore, who wishes to do God's commandment, but is unable, already possesses a good will, but as yet a small and weak one; he will, however, become able when he shall have acquired a great and robust will. When the martyrs did the great commandments which they obeyed, they acted by a great will, —that is, with great love. Of this love the Lord Himself thus speaks: "Greater love hath no man than this, that a man lay down his life for his friends." In accordance with this, the apostle also says, "He that loveth his neighbor hath fulfilled the law. For this: Thou shalt not commit adultery, Thou shalt not kill, Thou shalt not steal, Thou shalt not covet; and if there be any other commandment, it is briefly comprehended in this saying, namely, Thou shalt love thy neighbor as thyself. Love worketh no ill to his neighbor: therefore love is the fulfilling of the law." This love the Apostle Peter did not yet possess, when he for fear thrice denied the Lord. "There is no fear in love," says the Evangelist John in his first Epistle, "but perfect love casts out fear." But yet, however small and imperfect his love was, it was not wholly wanting when he said to the Lord, "I will lay down my life for Thy sake;" for he supposed himself able to affect what he felt himself willing to do. And who was it that had begun to give him his love, however small, but He who prepares the will, and perfects by His co-operation what He initiates by His operation? Forasmuch as in beginning He works in us that we may have the will, and in perfecting works with us when we have the will. On which account the apostle says, "I am confident of this very thing, that He which hath begun a good work in you will perform it until the day of Jesus Christ." He operates, therefore, without us, in order that we may will; but when we will, and so will that we may act, He co-operates with us. We can, however, ourselves do nothing to effect good works of piety without Him either working that we may will, or co-working when we will. Now, concerning His working that we may will, it is said: "It is God which worketh in you, even to will." While of His coworking with us, when we will and act by willing, the apostle says, "We know that in all things there is co-working for good to them that love God." What does this phrase, "all things," mean, but the terrible and cruel sufferings which affect our condition? That burden, indeed, of Christ, which is heavy for our infirmity, becomes light to love. For to such did the Lord say that His burden was light, as Peter was when he suffered for Christ, not as he was when he denied Him.

Chapter 34. —The Apostle's Eulogy of Love. Correction to Be Administered with Love.

This charity, that is, this will glowing with intense love, the apostle eulogizes with these words: "Who shall separate us from the love of Christ? shall tribulation, or distress, or persecution, or famine, or nakedness, or peril, or the sword? (As it is written, For Thy sake we are killed all the day long; we are accounted as sheep for the slaughter.) Nay, in all these things we are more than conquerors, through Him that loved us. For I am persuaded, that neither death, nor life, nor angels, nor principalities, nor things present, nor things to come, nor height, nor depth, nor any other creature, shall be able to separate us from the love of God, which is in Christ Jesus our Lord." And in another passage he says, "And yet I show unto you a more excellent way. Though I speak with the tongues of men and of angels, and have not love, I am become as sounding brass, or a tinkling cymbal. And though I have the gift of prophecy, and understand all mysteries, and all knowledge; and though I have all faith, so that I could remove mountains, and have not love, I am nothing. And though I bestow all my goods to feed the poor, and though I give my body to be burned, and have not love, it profited me nothing. Love suffered long, and is kind; love envies not; love vaunted not itself, is not puffed up, doth not behave itself unseemly, seeks not her own, is not easily provoked, thinks no evil; rejoices not in iniquity, but rejoiced in the truth; bears all things, believes all things, hopes all things, endures all things. Love never fails." And a little afterwards he says, "And now abides faith, hope, love, these three; but the greatest of these is love. Follow after love." He also says to the Galatians, "For, brethren, ye have been called unto liberty; only use not liberty for an occasion to the flesh, but by love serve one another. For all the law is fulfilled in one word, even in this, Thou shalt love thy neighbor as thyself." This is the same in effect as what he writes to the Romans: "He that loveth another hath fulfilled the law." In like manner he says to the Colossians, "And above all these things, put on love, which is the bond of perfectness." And to Timothy he writes, "Now the end of the commandment is love;" and he goes on to describe the quality of this grace, saying, "Out of a pure heart, and of a good conscience, and of faith unfeigned." Moreover, when he says to the Corinthians, "Let all your things be done with love," he shows plainly enough that even those chastisements which are deemed sharp and bitter by those who are corrected thereby, are to be administered with love. Accordingly, in another passage, after saying, "Warn them that are unruly, comfort the feeble-minded, support the weak, be patient toward all men," he immediately added, "See that none render evil for evil unto any man." Therefore, even when the unruly are corrected, it is not rendering evil for evil, but contrariwise, good. However, what but love worketh all these things?

Chapter 35. —Commendations of Love.

The Apostle Peter, likewise, says, "And, above all things, have fervent love among yourselves: for love shall cover the multitude of sins." The Apostle James also says, "If ye fulfil the royal law, according to the Scripture, Thou shalt love thy neighbor as thyself, ye do well." So also the Apostle John says, "He that loveth his brother abides in the right;" again, in another passage, "Whosoever doeth not righteousness is not of God, neither he that loveth not his brother; for this is the message which we have heard from the beginning, that we should love one another." Then he says again, "This is His commandment, that we should believe on the name of His Son Jesus Christ, and love one another." Once more: "And this commandment have we from Him that he who loveth God love his brother also." Then shortly afterwards he adds, "By this we know that we love the children of God, when we love God, and keep His commandments; for this is the love of God, that we keep His commandments: and His commandments are not grievous." While, in his second Epistle, it is written, "Not as though I wrote a new commandment unto thee, but that which we had from the beginning, that we love one another."

Chapter 36. —Love Commended by Our Lord Himself.

Moreover, the Lord Jesus Himself teaches us that the whole law and the prophets hang upon the two precepts of love to God and love to our neighbor. Concerning these two commandments the following is written in the Gospel according to St. Mark: "And one of the scribes came, and having heard them reasoning together, and perceiving that He had answered them well, asked Him: Which is the first commandment of all? And

Jesus answered him: The first of all the commandments is, Hear, O Israel! the Lord our God is one Lord; and thou shalt love the Lord thy God with all thine heart, and with all thy soul, and with all thy mind, and with all thy strength. This is the first commandment. And the second is like unto it: Thou shalt love thy neighbor as thyself. There is none other commandment greater than these." Also, in the Gospel according to St. John, He says, "A new commandment I give unto you, that ye love one another; as I have loved you, that ye also love one another. By this shall all men know that ye are my disciples, if ye have love to one another."

Chapter 37 [XVIII.]—The Love Which Fulfils the Commandments is Not of Ourselves, But of God.

All these commandments, however, respecting love or charity (which are so great, and such that whatever action a man may think he does well is by no means well done if done without love) would be given to men in vain if they had not free choice of will. But forasmuch as these precepts are given in the law, both old and new (although in the new came the grace which was promised in the old, but the law without grace is the letter which kills, but in grace the Spirit which giveth life), from what source is there in men the love of God and of one's neighbor but from God Himself? For indeed, if it be not of God but of men, the Pelagians have gained the victory; but if it come from God, then we have vanquished the Pelagians. Let, then, the Apostle John sit in judgment between us; and let him say to us, "Beloved, let us love one another." Now, when they begin to extol themselves on these words of John, and to ask why this precept is addressed to us at all if we have not of our own selves to love one another, the same apostle proceeds at once, to their confusion, to add, "For love is of God." It is not of ourselves, therefore, but it is of God. Wherefore, then, is it said, "Let us love one another, for love is of God," unless it be as a precept to our free will, admonishing it to seek the gift of God? Now, this would be indeed a thoroughly fruitless admonition if the will did not previously receive some donation of love, which might seek to be enlarged so as to fulfil whatever command was laid upon it. When it is said, "Let us love one another," it is law; when it is said, "For love is of God," it is grace. For God's "wisdom carries law and mercy upon her tongue." Accordingly, it is written in the Psalm, "For He who gave the law will give blessings."

Chapter 38. —We Would Not Love God Unless He First Loved Us. The Apostles Chose Christ Because They Were Chosen; They Were Not Chosen Because They Chose Christ.

Let no one, then, deceive you, my brethren, for we should not love God unless He first loved us. John again gives us the plainest proof of this when he says, "We love Him because He first loved us." Grace makes us lovers of the law; but the law itself, without grace, makes us nothing but breakers of the law. And nothing else than this is shown us by the words of our Lord when He says to His disciples, Ye have not chosen me, but I have chosen you." For if we first loved Him, in order that by this merit He might love us, then we first chose Him that we might deserve to be chosen by Him. He, however, who is the Truth says otherwise, and flatly contradicts this vain conceit of men. "You have not chosen me," He says. If, therefore, you have not chosen me, undoubtedly you have not loved me (for how could they choose one whom they did not love?). "But I," says He, "have chosen you." And then could they possibly help choosing Him afterwards, and preferring Him to all the blessings of this world? But it was because they had been chosen, that they chose Him; not because they chose Him that they were chosen. There could be no merit in men's choice of Christ, if it were not that God's grace was prevenient in His choosing them. Whence the Apostle Paul pronounces in the Thessalonians this benediction: "The Lord make you to increase and abound in love one toward another, and toward all men." This benediction to love one another He gave us, who had also given us a law that we should love each other. Then, in another passage addressed to the same church, seeing that there now existed in some of its members the disposition which he had wished them to cultivate, he says, "We are bound to thank God always for you, brethren, as it is meet, because that your faith grows exceedingly, and the charity of every one of you all toward each other abounds." This he said lest they should make a boast of the great good which they were enjoying from God, as if they had it of their own mere selves. Because, then, your faith has so great a growth (this is the purport of his words), and the love of every one of you all toward each other so greatly abounds, we ought to thank God concerning you, but not to praise you, as if you possessed these gifts of yourselves.

Chapter 39. —The Spirit of Fear a Great Gift of God.

The apostle also says to Timothy, "For God hath not given to us the spirit of fear, but of power, and of love, and of a sound mind." Now in respect of this passage of the apostle, we must be on our guard against supposing that we have not received the spirit of the fear of God, which is undoubtedly a great gift of God, and concerning which the prophet Isaiah says, "The Spirit of the Lord shall rest upon thee, the spirit of wisdom and understanding, the spirit of counsel and might, the spirit of knowledge and piety, the spirit of the fear of the Lord." It is not the fear with which Peter denied Christ that we have received the spirit of, but that fear concerning which Christ Himself says, "Fear Him who hath power to destroy both soul and body in hell; yea, I say unto you, Fear Him." This, indeed, He said, lest we should deny Him from the same fear which shook Peter; for such cowardice he plainly wished to be removed from us when He, in the preceding passage, said, "Be not afraid of them that kill the body, and after that have no more that they can do." It is not of this fear that we have received the spirit, but of power, and of love, and of a sound mind. And of this spirit the same Apostle Paul discourses to the Romans: "We glory in tribulations, knowing that tribulation worketh patience; and patience, experience; and experience, hope; and hope makes not ashamed; because the love of God is shed abroad in our hearts by the Holy Ghost, which is given unto us." Not by ourselves, therefore, but by the Holy Ghost which is given to us, does it come to pass that, through that very love, which he shows us to be the gift of God, tribulation does not do away with patience, but rather produces it. Again, he says to the Ephesians, "Peace be to the brethren, and love with faith." Great blessings these! Let him tell us, however, whence they come. "From God the Father," says he immediately afterwards, "and the Lord Jesus Christ." These great blessings, therefore, are nothing else than God's gifts to us.

Chapter 40 [XIX.]—The Ignorance of the Pelagians in Maintaining that the Knowledge of the Law Comes from God, But that Love Comes from Ourselves.

It is no wonder that light shines in darkness, and the darkness comprehended it not. In John's Epistle the Light declares, "Behold what manner of love the Father hath bestowed upon us, that we should be called the sons of God." And in the Pelagian writings the darkness says, "Love comes to us of our own selves." Now, if they only possessed the true, that is, Christian love, they would also know whence they obtained possession of it; even as the apostle knew when he said, "But we have received not the spirit of the world, but the Spirit which is of God, that we might know the things that are freely given to us of God." John says, "God is love." And thus the Pelagians affirm that they actually have God Himself, not from God, but from their own selves! and although they allow that we have the knowledge of the law from God, they will yet have it that love is from our very selves. Nor do they listen to the apostle when he says, "Knowledge puffed up, but love edifies." Now what can be more absurd, nay, what more insane and more alien from the very sacredness of love itself, than to maintain that from God proceeds the knowledge which, apart from love, puffs us up, while the love which prevents the possibility of this inflation of knowledge springs from ourselves? And again, when the apostle speaks of "the love of Christ as surpassing knowledge," what can be more insane than to suppose that the knowledge which must be subordinated to love comes from God, while the love which surpasses knowledge comes from man? The true faith, however, and sound doctrine declare that both graces are from God; the Scripture says, "From His face cometh knowledge and understanding;" and another Scripture says, "Love is of God." We read of "the Spirit of wisdom and understanding." Also of "the Spirit of power, and of love, and of a sound mind." But love is a greater gift than knowledge; for whenever a man has the gift of knowledge, love is necessary by the side of it, that he be not puffed up. For "love envies not, vaunted not itself, is not puffed up."

Chapter 41 [XX.]—The Wills of Men are So Much in the Power of God, that He Can Turn Them Whithersoever It Pleases Him.

I think I have now discussed the point fully enough in opposition to those who vehemently oppose the grace of God, by which, however, the human will is not taken away, but changed from bad to good, and assisted when it is good. I think, too, that I have so discussed the subject, that it is not so much I myself as the inspired Scripture which has spoken to you, in the clearest testimonies of truth; and if this divine record be looked into carefully, it shows us that not only men's good wills, which God Himself converts from bad ones, and, when converted by Him, directs to good actions and to eternal life, but also those which follow the world are so entirely at the disposal of God, that He turns them whithersoever He wills, and whensoever He wills,—to bestow kindness on some, and to heap punishment on others, as He Himself judges right by a counsel most secret to Himself, indeed, but beyond all doubt most righteous. For we find that some sins are even the punishment of other sins, as are those "vessels of wrath" which the apostle describes as "fitted to destruction;" as is also that hardening of Pharaoh, the purpose of which is said to be to set forth in him the power of God; as, again, is the flight of the Israelites from the face of the enemy before the city of Ai, for fear arose in their heart so that they fled, and this was done that their sin might be punished in the way it was right that it should be; by reason of which the Lord said to Joshua the son of Nun, "The children of Israel shall not be able to stand before the face of their enemies." What is the meaning of, "They shall not be able to stand"? Now, why did they not stand by free will, but, with a will perplexed by fear, took to flight, were it not that God has the lordship even over men's wills, and when He is angry turns to fear whomsoever He pleases? Was it not of their own will that the enemies of the children of Israel fought against the people of God, as led by Joshua, the son of Nun? And yet the Scripture says, "It was of the Lord to harden their hearts, that they should come against Israel in battle, that they might be exterminated." And was it not likewise of his own will that the wicked son of Gera cursed King David? And yet what says David, full of true, and deep, and pious wisdom? What did he say to him who wanted to smite the reviler? "What," said he, "have I to do with you, ye sons of Zeruiah? Let him alone and let him curse, because the Lord hath said unto him, Curse

David. Who, then, shall say, Wherefore hast thou done so?" And then the inspired Scripture, as if it would confirm the king's profound utterance by repeating it once more, tells us: "And David said to Abishai, and to all his servants, Behold, my son, which came forth from my bowels, seeks my life: how much more may this Benjamite do it! Let him alone, and let him curse; for the Lord hath bidden him. It may be that the Lord will look on my humiliation, and will requite me good for his cursing this day." Now what prudent reader will fail to understand in what way the Lord bade this profane man to curse David? It was not by a command that He bade him, in which case his obedience would be praiseworthy; but He inclined the man's will, which had become debased by his own perverseness, to commit this sin, by His own just and secret judgment. Therefore it is said, "The Lord said unto him." Now if this person had obeyed a command of God, he would have deserved to be praised rather than punished, as we know he was afterwards punished for this sin. Nor is the reason an obscure one why the Lord told him after this manner to curse David. "It may be," said the humbled king, "that the Lord will look on my humiliation, and will requite me good for his cursing this day." See, then, what proof we have here that God uses the hearts of even wicked men for the praise and assistance of the good. Thus did He make use of Judas when betraying Christ; thus did He make use of the Jews when they crucified Christ. And how vast the blessings which from these instances He has bestowed upon the nations that should believe in Him! He also uses our worst enemy, the devil himself, but in the best way, to exercise and try the faith and piety of good men, —not for Himself indeed, who knows all things before they come to pass, but for our sakes, for whom it was necessary that such a discipline should be gone through with us. Did not Absalom choose by his own will the counsel which was detrimental to him? And yet the reason of his doing so was that the Lord had heard his father's prayer that it might be so. Wherefore the Scripture says that "the Lord appointed to defeat the good counsel of Ahithophel, to the intent that the Lord might bring all evils upon Absalom." It called Ahithophel's counsel "good," because it was for the moment of advantage to his purpose. It was in favor of the son against his father, against whom he had rebelled; and it might have crushed him, had not the Lord defeated the counsel which Ahithophel had given, by acting on the heart of Absalom so that he rejected this counsel, and chose another which was not expedient for him.

Chapter 42 [XXI]—God Does Whatsoever He Wills in the Hearts of Even Wicked Men.

Who can help trembling at those judgments of God by which He does in the hearts of even wicked men whatsoever He wills, at the same time rendering to them according to their deeds? Rehoboam, the son of Solomon, rejected the salutary counsel of the old men, not to deal harshly with the people, and preferred listening to the words of the young men of his own age, by returning a rough answer to those to whom he should have spoken gently. Now whence arose such conduct, except from his own will? Upon this, however, the ten tribes of Israel revolted from him, and chose for themselves another king, even Jeroboam, that the will of God in His anger might be accomplished which He had predicted would come to pass. For what says the Scripture? "The king hearkened not unto the people; for the turning was from the Lord, that He might perform His saying, which the Lord spoke to Ahijah the Shilonite concerning Jeroboam the son of Nebat." All this, indeed, was done by the will of man, although the turning was from the Lord. Read the books of the Chronicles, and you will find the following passage in the second book: "Moreover, the Lord stirred up against Jehoram the spirit of the Philistines, and of the Arabians, that were neighbors to the Ethiopians; and they came up to the land of Judah, and ravaged it, and carried away all the substance which was found in the king's house." Here it is shown that God stirs up enemies to devastate the countries which He adjudges deserving of such chastisement. Still, did these Philistines and Arabians invade the land of Judah to waste it with no will of their own? Or were their movements so directed by their own will that the Scripture lies which tells us that "the Lord stirred up their spirit" to do all this? Both statements to be sure are true, because they both came by their own will, and yet the Lord stirred up their spirit; and this may also with equal truth be stated the other way: The Lord both stirred up their spirit, and yet they came of their own will. For the Almighty sets in motion even in the innermost hearts of men the movement of their will, so that He does through their agency whatsoever He wishes to perform through them, —even He who knows not how to will anything in unrighteousness. What, again, is the purport of that which the man of God said to King Amaziah: "Let not the army of Israel go with thee; for the Lord is not with Israel, even with all the children of Ephraim: for if thou shalt think to obtain with these, the Lord shall put thee to flight before thine enemies: for God hath power either to strengthen or to put to flight"? Now, how does the power of God help some in war by giving them confidence, and put others to flight by injecting fear into them, except it be that He who has made all things according to His own will, in heaven and on earth, also works in the hearts of men? We read also what Joash, king of Israel, said when he sent a message to Amaziah, king of Judah, who wanted to fight with him. After certain other words, he added, "Now tarry at home; why dost thou challenge me to thine hurt, that thou shouldest fall, even thou, and Judah with thee?" Then the Scripture has added this sequel: "But Amaziah would not hear; for it came of God, that he might be delivered into their hands, because they sought after the gods of Edom." Behold, now, how God, wishing to punish the sin of idolatry, wrought this in this man's heart, with whom He was indeed justly angry, not to listen to sound advice, but to despise it, and go to the battle, in which he with his army was routed. God says by the prophet Ezekiel, "If the prophet be deceived when he hath spoken a thing, I the Lord have deceived that prophet: I will stretch out my hand upon him, and will destroy him from the midst of my people Israel." Then there is the book of Esther, who was a woman of the people of Israel, and in the land of their captivity became the wife of the foreign King Ahasuerus. In this book it is written, that, being driven by necessity to interpose in behalf of her people, whom the king had ordered to be slain in every part of his dominions, she prayed to the Lord. So strongly was she urged by the necessity of the case, that she even ventured into the royal presence without the king's command, and contrary to her own custom. Now observe what the Scripture says: "He looked at her like a bull in the vehemence of his indignation; and the queen was afraid, and her color changed as she fainted; and she bowed herself upon the head of her delicate maiden which went before her. But God turned the king and transformed his indignation into gentleness." The Scripture says in the Proverbs of Solomon, "Even as the rush of water, so is the heart of a king in God's hand; He will turn it in whatever way He shall choose." Again, in the 104th Psalm, about the Egyptians, one reads what God did to them: "And He turned their heart to hate His people, to deal subtilty with His servants." Observe, likewise, what is written in the letters of the apostles. In the Epistle of Paul, the Apostle, to the Romans occur these words: "Wherefore God gave them up to uncleanness, through the lusts of their own hearts;" and a little afterwards: "For this cause God gave them up unto vile affections;" again, in the next passage: "And even as they did not like to retain God in their knowledge, God gave them over to a reprobate mind, to do those things which are not convenient." So also in his second Epistle to the Thessalonians, the apostle says of sundry persons, "Inasmuch as they received not the love of the truth, that they might be saved; therefore also God shall send them strong delusion, that they should believe a lie; that they all might be judged who believed not the truth, but had pleasure in unrighteousness."

Chapter 43. —God Operates on Men's Hearts to Incline Their Wills Whithersoever He Pleases.

From these statements of the inspired word, and from similar passages which it would take too long to quote in full, it is, I think, sufficiently clear that God works in the hearts of men to incline their wills whithersoever He wills, whether to good deeds according to His mercy, or to evil after their own deserts; His own judgment being sometimes manifest, sometimes secret, but always righteous. This ought to be the fixed and immoveable conviction of your heart, that there is no unrighteousness with God. Therefore, whenever you read in the Scriptures of Truth, that men are led aside, or that their hearts are blunted and hardened by God, never doubt that some ill deserts of their own have first occurred, so that they justly suffer these things. Thus you will not run counter to that proverb of Solomon: "The foolishness of a man perverted his ways, yet he blames God in his heart." Grace, however, is not bestowed according to men's deserts; otherwise grace would be no longer grace. For grace is so designated because it is given gratuitously. Now if God is able, either through the agency of angels (whether good ones or evil), or in any other way whatever, to operate in the hearts even of the wicked, in return for their deserts,—whose wickedness was not made by Him, but was either derived originally from Adam, or increased by their own will,—what is there to wonder at if, through the Holy Spirit, He works good in the hearts of the elect, who has wrought it that their hearts become good instead of evil?

Chapter 44 [XXII.]—Gratuitous Grace Exemplified in Infants.

Men, however, may suppose that there are certain good deserts which they think are precedent to justification through God's grace; all the while failing to see, when they express such an opinion, that they do nothing else than deny grace. But, as I have already remarked, let them suppose what they like respecting the case of adults, in the case of infants, at any rate, the Pelagians find no means of answering the difficulty. For these in receiving grace have no will; from the influence of which they can pretend to any precedent merit. We see, moreover, how they cry and struggle when they are baptized, and feel the divine sacraments. Such conduct would, of course, be charged against them as a great impiety, if they already had free will in use; and notwithstanding this, grace cleaves to them even in their resisting struggles. But most certainly there is no prevenient merit, otherwise the grace would be no longer grace. Sometimes, too, this grace is bestowed upon the children of unbelievers, when they happen by some means or other to fall, by reason of God's secret providence, into the hands of pious persons; but, on the other hand, the children of believers fail to obtain grace, some hindrance occurring to prevent the approach of help to rescue them in their danger. These things, no doubt, happen through the secret providence of God, whose judgments are unsearchable, and His ways past finding out. These are the words of the apostle; and you should observe what he had previously said, to lead him to add such a remark. He was discoursing about the Jews and Gentiles, when he wrote to the Romans—themselves Gentiles—to this effect: "For as ye, in times past, have not believed God, yet have now obtained mercy through their unbelief; even so have these also now not believed, that through your mercy they also may obtain mercy; for God hath concluded them all in unbelief, that He might have mercy upon all." Now, after he had thought upon what he said, full of wonder at the certain truth of his own assertion, indeed, but astonished at its great depth, how God concluded all in unbelief that He might have mercy upon all,—as if doing evil that good might come,—he at once exclaimed, and said, "O the depth of the riches both of the wisdom and knowledge of God! how unsearchable are His judgments, and His ways past finding out!" Perverse men, who do not reflect upon these unsearchable judgments and untraceable ways, indeed, but are ever prone to censure, being unable to understand, have supposed the apostle to say, and censoriously gloried over him for saying, "Let us do evil, that good may come!" God forbid that the apostle should say so! But men, without understanding, have thought that this was in fact said, when they heard these words of the apostle: "Moreover, the law entered, that the offence might abound; but where sin abounded, grace did much more abound." But grace, indeed, effects this purpose—that good works should now be wrought by those who previously did evil; not that they should persevere in evil courses and suppose that they are recompensed with good. Their language, therefore, ought not to be: "Let us do evil, that good may come;" but: "We have done evil, and good has come; let us henceforth do good, that in the future world we may receive good for good, who in the present life are receiving good for evil." Wherefore it is written in the Psalm, "I will sing of mercy and judgment unto Thee, O Lord." When the Son of man, therefore, first came into the world, it was not to judge the world, but that the world through Him might be saved. And this dispensation was for mercy; by and by, however, He will come for judgment—to judge the quick and the dead. And yet even in this present time salvation itself does not eventuate without judgment—although it be a hidden one; therefore He says, "For judgment I am come into this world, that they which see not may see, and that they which see may be made blind."

Chapter 45 [XXIII]—The Reason Why One Person is Assisted by Grace, and Another is Not Helped, Must Be Referred to the Secret Judgments of God.

You must refer the matter, then, to the hidden determinations of God, when you see, in one and the same condition, such as all infants unquestionably have,—who derive their hereditary evil from Adam,—that one is assisted so as to be baptized, and another is not assisted, so that he dies in his very bondage; and again, that one baptized person is left and forsaken in his present life, who God foreknew would be ungodly, while another baptized person is taken away from this life, "lest that wickedness should alter his understanding;" and be sure that you do not in such cases ascribe unrighteousness or unwisdom to God, in whom is the very fountain of righteousness and wisdom, but, as I have exhorted you from the commencement of this treatise, "whereto you have already attained, walk therein," and "even this shall God reveal unto you,"—if not in this life, yet certainly in the next, "for there is nothing covered that shall not be revealed." When, therefore, you hear the Lord say, "I the Lord have deceived that prophet," and likewise what the apostle says: "He hath mercy on whom He will have mercy, and whom He will He hardened," believe that, in the case of him whom He permits to be deceived and hardened, his evil deeds have deserved the judgment; whilst in the case of him to whom He shows mercy, you should loyally and unhesitatingly recognize the grace of the God who "rendered not evil for evil; but contrariwise blessing." Nor should you take away from Pharaoh free will, because in several passages God says, "I have hardened Pharaoh;" or," I have hardened or I will harden Pharaoh's heart;" for it does not by any means follow that Pharaoh did not, on this account, harden his own heart. For this, too, is said of him, after the removal of the fly plague from the Egyptians, in these words of the Scripture: "And Pharaoh hardened his heart at this time also; neither would he let the people go." Thus it was that both God hardened him by His just judgment, and Pharaoh by his own free will. Be ye then well assured that your labor will never be in vain, if, setting before you a good purpose, you persevere in it to the last. For God, who fails to render, according to their deeds, only to those whom He liberates, will then "recompense every man according to his works." God will, therefore, certainly recompense both evil for evil, because He is just; and good for evil, because He is good; and good for good, because He is good and just; only, evil for good He will never recompense, because He is not unjust. He will, therefore, recompense evil for evil—punishment for unrighteousness; and He will recompense good for evil—grace for unrighteousness; and He will recompense good for good—grace for grace.

Chapter 46 [XXIV.]—Understanding and Wisdom Must Be Sought from God.

Peruse attentively this treatise, and if you understand it, give God the praise; but where you fail to understand it, pray for understanding, for God will give you understanding. Remember what the Scriptures say: "If any of you lack wisdom, let him ask of God, who giveth to all men liberally, and upbraideth not; and it shall be given to him." Wisdom itself cometh down from above, as the Apostle James himself tells us. There is, however, another wisdom, which you must repel from you, and pray against its remaining in you; this the same apostle expressed his detestation of when he said, "But if ye have bitter envying and strife in your hearts, . . . this is not the wisdom which descended from above, but is earthly, sensual, devilish. For wherever there is envying and strife, there is also confusion, and every evil work. But the wisdom which is from above is first pure, then peaceable, gentle, and easy to be entreated, full of mercy and good works, without partiality, and without hypocrisy." What blessing, then, will that man not have who has prayed for this wisdom and obtained it of the Lord? And from this you may understand what grace is; because if this wisdom were of ourselves, it would not be from above; nor would it be an object to be asked for of the God who created us. Brethren, pray ye for us also, that we may live "soberly, righteously, and godly in this present world; looking for that blessed hope, and the glorious appearing of our Lord and Savior Jesus Christ," to whom belong the honor, and the glory, and the kingdom, with the Father and the Holy Ghost, for ever and ever. Amen.

www.ingramcontent.com/pod-product-compliance
Lightning Source LLC
Chambersburg PA
CBHW052111070526
44584CB00017B/2441